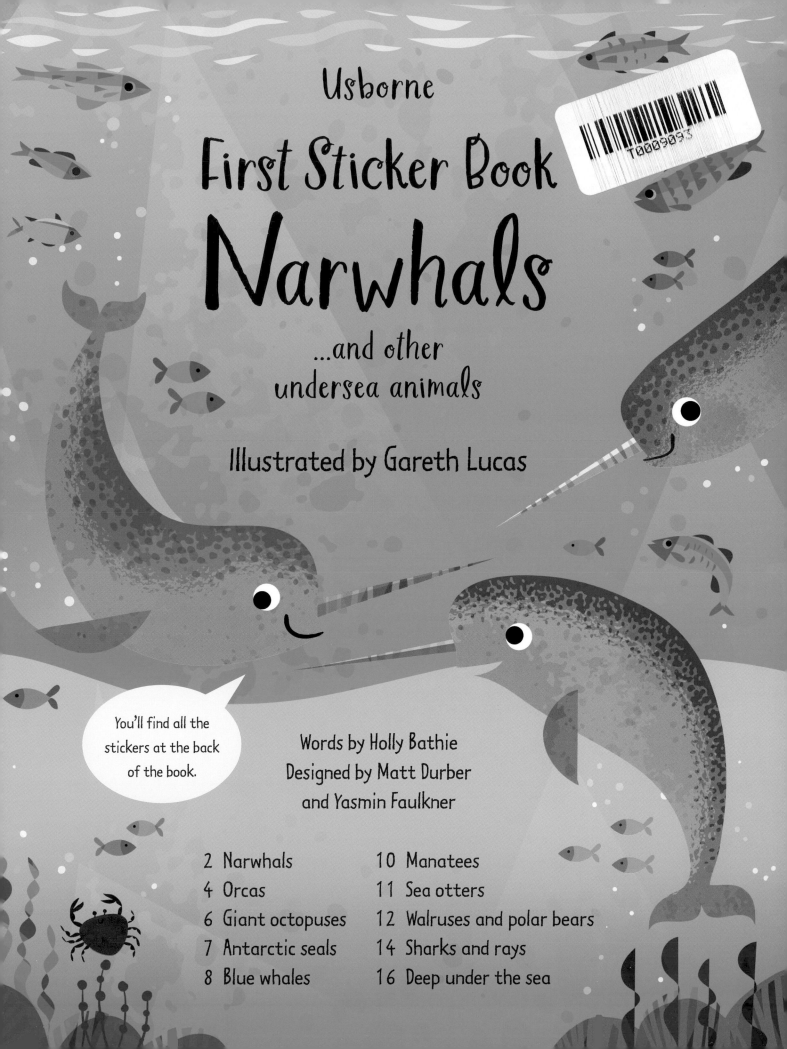

Usborne

First Sticker Book
Narwhals
...and other undersea animals

Illustrated by Gareth Lucas

You'll find all the stickers at the back of the book.

Words by Holly Bathie
Designed by Matt Durber
and Yasmin Faulkner

Narwhals

Narwhals are small whales that live in the Arctic Ocean, near the North Pole. Their unusual long 'horn' is actually a tusk, or tooth! Fill the icy sea with playful narwhals. Add more fish, and put some ringed seals on the ice.

Arctic char

Arctic
skuas

Orcas

These huge orcas (sometimes called killer whales), can be found in Arctic waters, along with narwhals. They are very social, and live together in family groups, called 'pods'. Add a pod of orcas to the scene.

Arctic terns

5

Giant octopuses

Giant Pacific octopuses can be found hiding in kelp forests, which are underwater areas of tall kelp seaweed. Stick two octopuses here, and find a place for a bat ray among the kelp.

Kelp

Sea urchins

Antarctic seals

Lots of different kinds of seals live in the Antarctic, near the South Pole. Elephant seals have large noses, leopard seals have spotted skin, and fur seals are furry! Put more of these seals in the water.

Blue whales

Around Greenland, enormous blue whales can be spotted swimming alongside narwhals and beluga whales, which are much smaller and also known as 'white whales' because they are so pale. Find a space for all of these whales in the cold water.

Blue whales are the largest animal
on the planet, and every day
they eat tons and tons of tiny
creatures called krill.

Manatees

Manatees are large, gentle-looking sea mammals, sometimes known as 'sea cows'. West Indian manatees can be found around coral reefs. Add them to this scene, along with lots of bright tropical fish and sea turtles.

Sea otters

These playful sea otters live by the Californian coast.
They like to rest together on their backs in groups, called 'rafts'.
Add a raft of sea otters here, and more crabs for them to eat.

Walruses and polar bears

Walruses and polar bears are large Arctic animals that spend a lot of their time resting on the ice. Walruses have long tusks and whiskers – add some more here. Stick on some fishing polar bears, too.

Sharks and rays

Silky sharks and reef manta rays sweep around these coastal waters in the Indian Ocean. Stick them on here, and add lots of flying fish for the sharks to catch.

Deep under the sea

All sorts of weird and wonderful creatures live deep under the sea. Find a place for another giant squid, then add lots more fish and eels.

Orcas pages 4-5

Orcas

Arctic terns

Arctic cod

Narwhal

Giant octopuses page 6

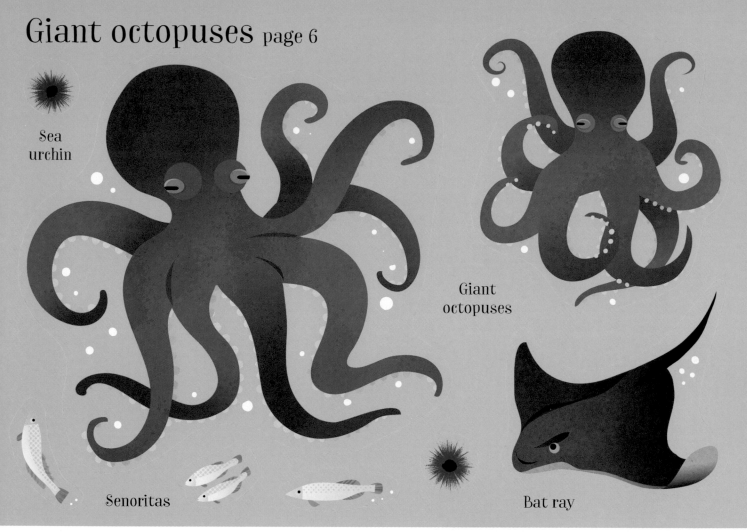

Sea urchin

Giant octopuses

Senoritas

Bat ray

Antarctic seals page 7

Elephant seals

Antarctic silverfish

Leopard seals

Fur seal

Blue whales

Beluga whales

Narwhals

Blue whales

Krill

Manatees page 10

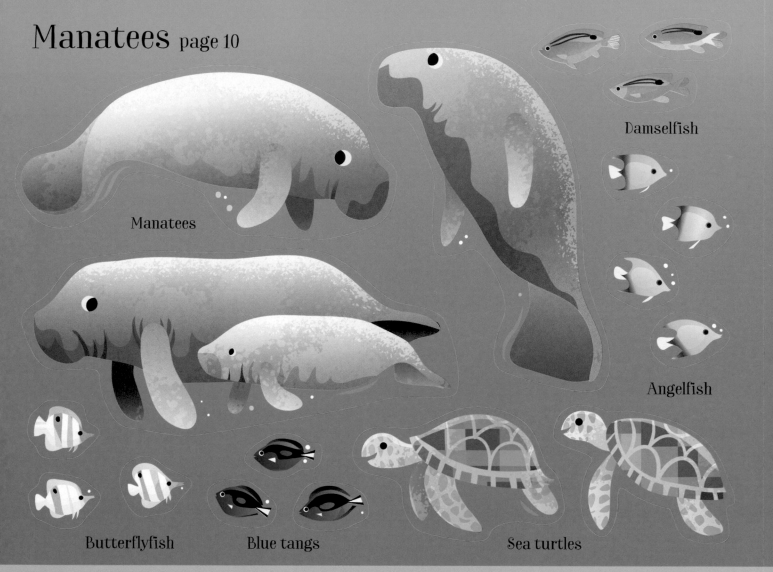

Manatees

Damselfish

Angelfish

Butterflyfish

Blue tangs

Sea turtles

Sea otters page 11

Dungeness crabs

Walruses and polar bears pages 12-13

Kittiwakes

Arctic cod

Walruses

Narwhal

Polar bear

Sharks and rays pages 14-15

Flying
fish

Silky sharks

Leatherback
turtle

Manta ray

Gulper eels

Marine
hatchetfish

Giant squid

Angler
fish

Deep-sea eelpout

Lanternfish